THE MAGIC OF HOME

How to find Joy in Living Simply

Melanie Steele

INTRODUCTION

It's often said that home is where the heart is, and that home is a sanctuary. During the lockdown years, I think many people realised the importance of the latter. When we were confined to our homes, or when we moved to working from home being a common place occurrence I think we all experienced a shift in our thinking. Home was no longer just somewhere we slept and ate. It was somewhere we worked, schooled children, ate all our meals. Even now in 2024 when the days of lockdown are behind us, many of us are still adjusting to a new normal- which includes redefining the space we call home.

As someone who is a self confessed homebody, I'm always looking for new ways and inspiration to make my home a sanctuary. A space that is warm, welcoming and ultimately a space that I want to be, and refreshes me. A space where I can be me. A space that works for me, and most importantly, *feels* like me (and my husband too of course!)

This book is divided into two parts.

Part one is the "how to" section with my tips and tricks for living simply, sustainably and on a budget. This is the reference section-where you can find information on a topic you're particularly interested in.

Part two is a collection of thoughts and reflections in a diary type format. This is where you can see how I "walk my talk". I didn't want this to be a dry book filled with *just* tips and instructions. There are plenty of those out there already.

After all "Show, don't tell" is pivotal to writing a book that someone wants to read!

PART I

CHAPTER ONE

I am an early bird- each day you'll find me awake somewhere between 6.00 and 6.30am. I have the odd Saturday where I might sleep until 7:00, but that's rare. My husband is most definitely not an early bird, but that's ok- it means I get a good hour to myself on weekends, maybe a half hour during the week when he has to get up for work.

Coffee is life. The first thing I do is go over to my Nespresso machine and set it going. Fresh water in the tank, a new coffee pod and Almond Milk in the milk frother. I wait until all the buttons stop flashing, hit the latte one and it whirs into action. I don't know why, but my machine does a better job at frothing Almond milk than Oat milk, so that's what I use.

Whilst I'm waiting, I open the curtains and see what the world looks like today. If it's bright and sunny that's an instant Dopamine hit- this is England, we don't get many days like that! More often than not its overcast and grey which doesn't give me the dopamine hit, but nonetheless- it's a new morning and that is something to be grateful for. I take a moment to enjoy the calm- in an hour or so many of my neighbours will be on the school run and/or going to work and the silence will be broken up with the slamming of doors, and the dinging sound some cars seem to make when they first start up.

I sip my coffee and do the inevitable phone scroll. There are 2 things I do every morning on my phone without fail- I plant a tree for free using Treeapp, and I sync my Bellabeat health tracker to see how well I've slept overnight. Starting your day my planting a tree is far more preferable to doomscrolling on social media. I'll check Instagram if I can see my husband has sent me reels. I think the sending of reels should be added to the 5 Official Love Languages- he always sends me things that make me smile, or laugh, or both!

Once he's gone to work- whether that's' to his home office or the actual office, that's when my day begins. I work part time a couple of mornings a week, but other than that you'll find me at home- cleaning, cooking, baking. Or I might be out- wondering around Charity shops, picking up some fresh produce or perusing B&M's (If you know, you know!) But mostly- I'm home and doing everything needed to make it a cosy retreat from the world.

I used to work the typical 9-5, and I hated it. I'm introverted by nature and having to be with people all day every day was *stressful*. I've never been so glad as when I changed to a part time low stress job where I can work alone. For me it's the perfect balance- just enough time outside the home to stay sane and have a healthy coffee/books/trinkets fund- but not so much that I don't have time to do what needs doing at home. I recognise I'm incredibly fortunate to be in this position, but I don't rest on my laurels. I couldn't stand to be home and watch TV all day (not that we own one) or just sit and do nothing. Nope. That would not do. I love keeping house- and it means we can both just relax at the end of the day- everything's been done.

Whilst not everyone enjoys keeping house as much as I do- or has as much time to devote to it, I think we can all benefit from some sage advice on how to do it better, cheaper, and quicker. How to cook delicious healthy meals, stick to a budget and create a home that you can't wait to get back to after a long day, or don't want to leave if you're home like I am!

I'll also be sharing how living life at home can be wonderful, and simple. After all- life is not about cleaning and cooking 24/7- even if it feels like it (I'm sure busy mums can relate here) Your home should be a place to relax, have fun and find rest too. Having fun at home simplifies life, and saves money too- bonus!

Essentially, living a simple life and saving money go hand in hand, and I'll be exploring that later on in this book.

CHAPTER TWO

DISCONNECTING

I have a friend who loves sending me posts and reels about life in the 90'/00s. And I love to watch and read them! It got me thinking. Was it just pure nostalgia that made me love these posts? Or something more?

I am an elder millennial- the last generation that remembers life before the internet. It wasn't even that long ago, but it feels it. The internet changed everything, and continues to do so. Don't get me wrong- I love the internet. So much information and entertainment at your finger tips. But that's also the reason that I dislike it- there's just *too much,* and a lot of it is negative.

Take the news for example. It used to be you would watch it in the morning, or if not the morning you'd watch it with dinner, or later on in the evening. But now? The news is

24/7. It never stops. News websites update their headlines all day everyday, and it can get intense.

I'm not saying that you should go live in a cave and never read a news headline ever again. Ignorance is not always bliss. I do think though that a key part of keeping life simple is allowing ourselves the freedom to be disconnected- even for short periods of time. Being disconnected was one of the key things that stood out for me as to why I love the nostalgia of the 90s/00s. I had a mobile phone at 15, but I wasn't expected to live with it stuck to my hand, and answer every message in 10 seconds. It didn't have the internet, or email. I could communicate with my friends and family, but I wasn't on it 24/7. I was still going out and hanging out with friends, being a teenager.

If that's a feeling you want back- then claim it. My phone has been on silent/do not disturb for over a decade (Because I'm a millennial and I hate phone calls) I have emergency bypass set up for necessary contacts. But other than that, I do my best to not be on it as much as possible. I limit social media scrolling, and I read the headlines once a day. That's enough for me!

CHAPTER THREE

SIMPLIFY AND SAVE

Where I live, the average detached house will set you back over £800,000. Yikes. We do not live in a detached house, but it's still expensive. We are fortunate to be home owners, but I'm not going to say that we achieved that because we stopped drinking take away coffee and eating Avocado toast (I hate Avocados FYI) because that would be a complete lie. Home ownership is out of reach for many and that angers me. Especially when people make ridiculous suggestions to save money like the ones I just mentioned. Unless you inherit money, can live at home indefinitely for next to nothing, make a good salary and have a partner also earning good money- it's next to impossible to achieve home ownership.

Whilst you may not have a lot of control over the cost of your rent or mortgage, there are other ways to keep things more affordable as I have discovered over the years. When I went part time I felt a sense of needing to do all I could, within reason, to keep costs down. It's not that we were wild spenders before- far from it. But it was important that we minimised our costs seeing as though the overall household income was less.

In doing so, I realised that one of the side effects of being more conscious of our money was that life became more simple. The magic of home, and indeed life, is keeping it simple.

<u>Simple things that bring me joy and save money</u>

I'll go over these in more depth later, but here's the basics to inspire you!

Making my own coffee each morning. It

always tastes good, and it costs pennies! I only buy takeaway coffee a handful of times each year- most notably when Starbucks brings back the Pumpkin Spice Latte. Its a little annual treat to go out and enjoy that first taste of Autumn.

Baking my own Bread. I bought a used bread maker for £10 and its a game changer! Simply pop everything in, press a button and that's it! Delicious home baked bread. I do buy bread from the supermarket- as we need it to last a few days. But come the weekend there is nothing better than freshly baked bread. You can even set a timer so its ready when you wake up.

Scratch Cooking- There is something so satisfying about taking a bunch of ingredients and turning it into something delicious. Even if its as simple as making your own pasta sauce! You can save a lot of money cooking this way, and it will benefit your health too.

Menu Planning- Goes hand in hand with the above. Yes, you've heard this tip a million times. It's because it works, but few people do it. For 2 adults we spend about £200 a month on food. That's pretty low by most peoples standards- and it's because I plan every meal 2 weeks at a time! Also, we are vegetarians which definitely helps as meat is expensive, but we don't buy faux meat products very often either as those are just as expensive. We stick to supermarket own brands with a few exceptions (Tea and Coffee we are *very* particular about, for example) We don't buy alcohol, fizzy pop or convenience foods either.

Reading - I have a gorgeous purple armchair and footstool in our spare room sat next to a small table. I love to light a candle, grab a book and read! There's a blanket too for when the weather is cooler. You might not have a room to dedicate to this, but you could set up a little corner in another room to have as your reading nook.

You can easily save on books by going to your local library, or buying them used. You might not be able to get the latest releases right away, but you'll find tons of other great books while you wait.

Visiting local parks and beauty spots- who needs an expensive day out at an attraction when you can spend time out in nature? We do have a National Trust membership, but you don't need one to enjoy local woodland. Pack a picnic, fill a thermos with tea, grab a blanket and you have the makings of a great day.

Other general things include minimal use of heating, not wasting water (use eco cycles for everything!) I have a pay as you go Sim, and we don't upgrade mobile phones unless they stop working.

CHAPTER FOUR

KEEPING IT CLEAN

You're not going to enjoy being at home if it's in a state of dissaray. Keeping your home clean and tidy is the best way to maintain its sanctuary like feel. It doesn't have to consume your entire day, and it certainly doesn't have to be perfect.

I'll admit- there are days when I'm more motivated to clean than others. Sometimes I just want to write on my blog, or watch an episode or two of something. And there are days that definitely happens. If you're at home most of the time- you absolutely need something for *you*. Something creative, fun and inspiring. But more on that later.

I feel like cleaning has taken on a life of its own on social media- #cleanwithme, cleantok, cleaning influencers- it's content that people like to consume. I'm reliably informed that some people like to watch cleaning videos on YouTube whilst they clean their own homes- they find it motivating. Personally that's not for me- but if it works for you, that's great!

A word of caution- you do not need the 5000 products that cleaning influencers are trying to sell you. Or personalised bottles. The basics will suffice! Think about it- your grandparents did just fine with what they had.

All you need:

Washing up liquid
Cloths
Scrubbing Brush (I like Scrub Mummy)
Mop
Cheap toothbrushes (For fiddly bits)
Disinfectant
Bathroom cleaner
All purpose spray

I like to have set days for things- One day for

Bathroom and Bedrooms, One day for Kitchen and Living Room, and Saturday is laundry day. Some people divide by task-dusting one day, mopping another, etc. But I prefer the concept of finishing an entire room at once. It feels more complete to do all the tasks in one room for me.

It you stay on top of things it will eventually become quicker each time so if you're starting with a particularly messy space it will seem daunting- but tackling it each week will get easier!

Deep cleaning is also needed- things like pulling out furniture, the forgotten baseboards, the inside of the fridge. I recommend writing a list of these jobs- ideally on your phone, and keeping track of when you last did it.

CHAPTER FIVE

SCRATCH COOKING

Food, transport and mortgage/rent are the biggest costs most of us incur. We might not be able to rent somewhere cheaper, or reduce the mortgage, or downsize. We might work/live in an area with poor transport links that means we have to use a car- or the reverse, somewhere where you *have* to travel by public transport (Say, into London) and it costs a fortune.

What we can potentially have some control over is how much we spend on food.

STOCK YOUR PANTRY

Stocking your pantry is one of the best ways to keep your food spend low. If you have all the basics, you can whip up almost anything. Conversely, if all you have is random odds and ends, or ready made good for one dinner options- you're more limited, and will likely have to run to the supermarket to get what you need. All those little trips add up!

Here's a pantry list to get you started:

Dry Goods

Oats
Plain Flour
Bread Flour (If you bake your own bread!)
Cornflour
Rice
Baking Powder
Bicarbonate of Soda
Sugar- White and Brown
Chocolate Chips

Herbs and Spices

Basil
Oregano
Paprika

Cumin
Chilli Powder
Garlic Powder
Onion Powder
Bouillon/Stock Cubes
Rice vinegar (for Chinese inspired dishes)
Sesame oil

Tins/Other

Tomato Puree
Passata or Chopped Tomatoes

Chickpeas
Baked Beans
Black Beans

Frozen

Vegetables- Peas, Sweetcorn, Broccoli,
Carrots, etc.
Diced Onions (Lifesaver!)

Obviously these will be supplemented by
fresh food such as milk, butter, eggs and

produce, but having these on hand gives you lots of options to turn those fresh items into a great meal.

Breadmaker Recipes

Use Basic Bake programme for these, size Large unless otherwise stated. Put the ingredients in the pan in the order they are written in, unless your machine manual says otherwise.

I have had great success using Flora Unsalted Plant Butter in place of dairy butter in these recipes if you want/need it to be vegan. Egg replacer should work just fine as well.

<u>White Bread</u>

1tsp Yeast
475g White Bread Flour
1.5tsp Sugar
25g Butter
1 1/4tsp Salt

320ml Water

Brown Bread

1tsp Yeast
475g Wholemeal Bread Flour
1.5tsp Sugar
25g Butter
1 1/4tsp Salt
320ml Water

Maple Pecan Loaf

Use the Raisin/Dispenser setting so the machine mixes in the pecans at the right time.

3/4tsp Yeast
200g White Bread Flour
200g Wholemeal Bread Flour
15g Butter
1tsp Salt
3tbsp Maple Syrup
280ml Water
75g Pecans, chopped and placed in

dispenser.

Spicy Fruit Loaf

1tsp Yeast

400g Wholemeal Bread Flour

2tsp Sugar

75g Butter

1tsp Salt

2 Eggs, Medium (Can use egg replacer)

2tsp Cinnamon

1tsp Mixed Spice

120ml Water

120ml Milk (Can be plant based)

150g Mixed Dried Fruit, placed in dispenser.

Dough Recipes

Use the dough setting- on my machine this is the pizza setting. (If only it made the whole pizza!)

Pizza Dough

1/2tsp Yeast

300g Bread Flour (White or Brown)
1 tbsp Olive Oil
1tsp Salt
170ml Water

Once dough Is made, divide into 2 balls. Leave to prove for one hour. Roll out on a floured work surface, top with sauce and cheese then bake on a pizza tray at 200/Gas 6 for 15-20mins.

Only want 1 pizza? Roll out the dough and bake one for 5 minutes. Allow to cool, then wrap tightly and freeze. Can be used straight from frozen.

Cheats tip- place a Pyrex dish filled with boiling water on the bottom of the oven. Pop the dough balls on a pizza tray on the top shelf. Close the door and come back to perfectly puffed up dough!

Cinnamon Buns

1tsp Yeast

250g White Bread Flour

1tsp Sugar

25g Butter (Can be plant based)

1 tbsp Milk (Can be plant based)

½ tsp Salt

1 Egg, medium (Can use egg replacer)

100ml Water

For The Filling

28g Butter, softened (Use hard plant based butter if making vegan, not spread)

50g Brown Sugar

1tsp Cinnamon

Once the dough is made, roll it out on a lightly floured work surface to a rectangle approx 26cm x 20cm.

Spread the filling on to the dough, then roll it up from the long edge, as tightly as you can. Slice it into 8 (Use a serrated knife OR dental floss for a clean cut) and place into a lightly oiled tin and leave to prove until well risen.

DON'T do the cheats pizza dough prove here- we don't want the butter to melt! Leave them at room temperature.

Bake at 220/Gas 7 for 15-20mins until golden.

Once cooled, drizzle with glacé icing (Icing sugar mixed with either a few drops of water or milk)

Variation- Chelsea Buns

Swap the Cinnamon In the filling for Mixed Spice, and add in 100g of Mixed Dried Fruit.

Breakfast Ideas

Waffle/Pancake Mix

150g Plain Flour
1 Egg
300ml Milk

2tbsp Vegetable Oil
1tbsp Sugar
2tsp Baking Powder
Pinch of Salt

Waffles- Mix everything together in a bowl until smooth. Preheat your waffle maker, then pour in the mix once it's ready. I get 4 big waffles from this, but you may get more if you're waffle maker is smaller.

Pancakes- Mix everything together in a bowl until smooth. Drop 3-4tbsp of mix per pancake into a hot frying pan. Use silicone egg rings if you want them perfectly round! Once bubbles appear, flip gently and cook the other side. Use the oven to keep them warm.

Both the waffles and pancakes can be frozen- or placed in the fridge to be eaten within a day or two. If freezing, allow to defrost fully before reheating.

3 Ways with Oats

Classic Porridge

40g Oats
200ml Milk
1tbsp Flaxseed (Optional)

Heat gently on the stove until thick, or cover and microwave for a few minutes.

Toppings- Golden Syrup (the taste of childhood!) Maple Syrup, Cinnamon, Nuts, Chopped Fruit.

Overnight Oats

40g Oats
200ml Milk
1Tbsp Maple Syrup (or to taste)
1tbsp Flaxseed (Optional)

Flavour Combinations

Reese's- Add 1tbsp cocoa, 1tbsp peanut butter, and 1tsp vanilla.

Cookie Dough- Add 1tbsp almond butter, 2tbsp choc chips.

Apple Pie- Add ½ small apple grated and 1tsp cinnamon

Blueberry Lemon- A handful of blueberries, 1-2tsp lemon zest.

Banana Bread- ½ a banana, chopped. 1Tsp vanilla, 1tsp cinnamon.

Make up your preferred flavour, place in a sealed container in the fridge overnight- and enjoy your ready made breakfast!

Baked Oats

This one is for the oat haters who dislike the texture of cooked/soaked oats. Baking oats makes them more cake like, and entirely different from porridge or overnight oats.

40g rolled oats

½ tsp baking powder,
2 tsp maple syrup
1 egg
1 small or ½ large banana

Preheat the oven to 180c/ gas 4.

Pop all the ingredients into a blender, and blend until smooth.

Pour into a ramekin or a mini pie dish and bake for 25-30 minutes, or until well risen and a skewer comes out clean when inserted.

You can use any of the flavour combinations fro earlier- just don't add chocolate chips until after you've blended!

Lunch/Dinner Basics

Here is a selection of basic sauces that you can make from your pantry instead of buying ready made. I've included 5 here to get you started, but there's lots more online!

Tomato Sauce

Can be used for bolognese, pasta, lasagne, etc!

2 tbsp Oil
500g Passata (or chopped tomatoes)
1 onion, chopped
1-2 cloves garlic, chopped
1 carrot, chopped
1 celery stick, chopped
1 bay leaf
1/2-1 tsp sugar

Fry the onion and garlic until softened. Add in the other vegetables and cook until softened, about 10-15minutes. Finally, add the tomatoes, sugar and bay leaf. Simmer for 30mins or so until thickened. You can leave as is, or puree for a smooth sauce.

You can easily double this recipe to feed more people or if you're batch cooking.

Curry Sauce

2 tbsp vegetable oil
500g onion, diced
6 garlic cloves, peeled and chopped
1 tsp ginger paste, or root ginger peeled
and chopped
2 tbsp curry paste of your choice
500g passata OR 400g chopped tomatoes

Fry the onion and garlic until softened. Add
in the ginger and cook for 1-2mins, then add
in the curry paste. Cook for another minute.
Add 1 litre of water, the tomatoes and 1 tsp
salt and bring to a boil. Reduce heat slightly,
and cook for a further 10mins until
thickened.

Stir Fry Sauce

75ml soy sauce
1 tbsp sesame oil
1 tsp Chinese rice vinegar
3 tsp runny honey OR agave nectar
3 garlic cloves, peeled and crushed
pinch dried chilli flakes

Stir everything together, then use in your stir fry!

Sweet and Sour Sauce

200ml pineapple juice
100g light brown soft sugar
4 tbsp tomato ketchup
2 tbsp soy sauce
3 tbsp rice wine vinegar
1 tbsp cornflour

Put all ingredients except cornflour in a small saucepan, and whisk well. Bring to a simmer. Add 1tbsp water to the cornflour, mix it up then add to the saucepan. Whisk everything together until thickened.

Basic Hummus

Ok- NOT a sauce, but you can definitely make hummus pasta, so I'm including it here!

1 can chickpeas, drained

60ml water
2 cloves garlic, peeled and crushed
1 lemon juiced, half zested
3 tbsp tahini

Thoroughly drain and rinse the chickpeas. Add to a blender with water and blend until almost smooth. Add the rest of the ingredients, and blend until smooth. You can add up to 30ml more water if the consistency is too thick, but only add a little at a time in case it gets too runny!

Tofu/Tempeh

Tofu/tempeh are great sources of protein on a vegetarian or vegan diet- for the days when beans just won't cut it! Here are two easy ways to prepare them for adding to a dish.

Air Fryer Tofu

1 block tofu
3 tbsp cornflour

Press tofu if you haven't brought it pre pressed.
Cut into cubes and roll in the cornflour.

Tip- Chinese 5 spice makes a great addition here if you're using your tofu in a chinese inspired dish.

Preheat air fryer to 190c.
Cook for 10mins. Have a look- cook for an additional 5mins if it doesn't look crispy enough.

Tempeh Marinading

Tempeh, like tofu, can take on any flavour you like! The key is to slice and marinade it for 24hrs beforehand.

If you're after a cheaper fake bacon alternative, try this recipe!

"Bacon" marinade

60ml Soy Sauce
2 tsp liquid smoke (Amazon!)
2 tbsp maple syrup

Slice your tempeh. Stir marinade ingredients together and pour over your slices. Keep in a sealed container in the fridge overnight.

Next day- preheat oven to 180c/Gas 4. Bake for 20mins, turning halfway through and adding some extra mariande.

Alternatively- fry it in a pan until crispy!

<u>Simple Lunch/Dinner Ideas</u>

- Jacket potato with topping of choice
- Stir Fry with Noodles
- Spaghetti Bolognese with Lentils
- Tomato Pasta with Vegetables (Add chillis to the sauce for spice)
- Air fryer Tofu with sauce of choice and rice
- Vegetable Curry (Potatoes and Root Veg work great here)

- Tempeh Sandwich (Tons of marinade ideas online)
- Hummus with pitta and/or crudities

These are simple ideas to get you started- I didn't want this to become a super long recipe book -so consider this inspiration for your own scratch cooking ideas!

CHAPTER SIX

FREE ENTERTAINMENT

Living a simple life doesn't have to be boring. You aren't required to live as if you were in a secluded religious order. In fact, you aren't required to do *anything*. If you want to spend your hard earned cash on concert tickets or a weekend away, that is your prerogative.

However, I suspect if you're reading this book that you are yearning for a more simple life- one that doesn't require pressing refresh every 0.1seconds on Ticketmaster to buy those expensive concert tickets, only to realise they are all gone in an hour.

So, for those of us looking to simplify, but still enjoy our lives- what does that mean? It means getting creative, and getting local.

Start with local parks, woodland and/or

forests. These are a great way to get out of the house, and don't cost a thing. Take in the beauty of it all- or make it more fun by challenging yourself to name all the different kinds of trees or birds. I admit, I'm still not very good at this. I can show you an Oak, A Silver Birch and a Beech tree- everything else is a bit of a blur. But hey, I can keep learning. There are some great apps out there to help you identify these things, or you can go old school with a book from the library.

Keeping it local- how long has it been since you checked what was going on where you live in terms of events/days out? Your local paper, council website, village notice-board or local Facebook groups are all great sources of information as that's where local events tend to be advertised- it makes sense, right? For example, our local garden centre is having a spring market this weekend. There will be stalls selling food, crafts, jewellery- all sorts. The trick is of course not to spend all your money. If you do spend some, at least you are supporting local business- which is always a plus.

Farmers markets are another good one- they have way more than just produce these days. They also have produce that is free from plastic and pesticides. They might even have produce you've never seen for sale in the supermarket- because it's not popular enough to sell there, or cost prohibitive to stock.

Now then-this book is called The Magic of Home, so what can we do at home that is fun and free, or at least cheap? Lots actually!

Reading is the top of my list- and you can get books for free from the library so you don't have to go crazy on Amazon and have a ton of new books delivered the next day.

Writing- I'm writing this book, you could too-if writing is something that interests you! Whether you like writing stories, poems, even screenplays. So long as you have a computer or laptop, you can write to your hearts content. If you don't have MS Office and don't want to pay, download Libre Office. It's free, and what I use. You can also use Grammarly for free online to check your work. If you fancy having a go at self publishing, it's free and easy to do via Amazon. Search KDP Publishing to get all the information.

Board Games- Disclaimer here. If you're buying anything other than Monopoly/Cluedo sorts of games, they can be expensive. Its worth having a look online or in local charity shops to find board games for a more affordable price. A cheap alternative is TTRPG'S (Table top role playing games) which you can often download and print for just a few pounds. Bonus- you are supporting independent creators. Check out itch.io for a great selection. So long as you have dice and playing cards, you're good to go for most of them- but do check before you buy. I highly recommend The Librarians Apprentice!

Inexpensive hobbies- Lets be real. Things like sewing, knitting and crochet can be costly. The materials, needles, possibly even machines. There are other hobbies with lower costs. Think adult colouring books (or kids ones if the tiny details in the adult ones terrify you) sketching (pad and a set of pencils) learning a new language (Duolingo is free) blogging (you can start for free and later buy a domain/hosting if you love it) or playing free games on the computer (Steam regularly has free games, and The Sims is free if you want a throwback to your 00s childhood) There's definitely others, but those are some suggestions to get you started.

Movies can be free or low cost if you rent DVD's from the library, or buy from a charity shop. Most of us however have at least one streaming service, so make the most of it!

Podcasts are two a penny, and if nothing else have yourself a one person dance party with a Spotify playlist.

I'm not saying you should never go to a concert/theatre/cinema/theme park or paid attraction ever again. But if you're after a simpler life, and want to have more money for what really matters to you- start having fun at home!

CHAPTER SEVEN

HOME DECOR

To live simply and affordably means learning to love life at home.

For me, I'd rather be home then almost anywhere (except maybe a nice holiday in the sun on occasion) Home is my happy place. It's where I drink delicious coffee, cook from scratch dinners, read in my comfy armchair- all the good things!

To love life at home, you need to make your home a place you want to be- if it isn't already. This doesn't mean automatically rushing out to Ikea and Dunelm and buying the place up. It's about taking your time to curate things, maybe even just moving the furniture around. It's about deciding what you really want it to be, and how it can work (better) for you.

Charity shops are your best friend here if you're working on a tight budget. You can find all sorts of hidden treasures in the home section. Paintings, crockery sets, vases- everything you need to make your home special without spending lots of money. You could also try Olio or Freecycle for free/low cost items. Car boots can also be a great way to find unique items.

Before you buy anything though, check Pinterest for inspiration- unless you already have a vision for what you want. Looking at different set ups and colour schemes is really useful for seeing how to achieve a certain look or style, rather than buying different things that you love individually- but maybe don't go together all that well. Unless you're going for a shabby chic look- you do you!

However, don't fall into the trap of wanting to recreate a room exactly. A lot of those rooms have been styled by interior designers who have a large budget and know exactly what they are doing. Inspiration, not copying, is the goal here. It's your home-make it your own!

Simple Ways To Make Your Home Cosy

Scented candles
Blankets In easy reach of the sofa
Rugs on wood/laminate floors
Make a Tea/Coffee station in a small area of your kitchen
Fill your walls with unique wallart/pictures
Greenery- faux greenery looks so realistic these days, but if you're blessed with a green thumb you can get houseplants fairly inexpensively

PART II

CHAPTER EIGHT

LAUNDRY TALES

It's Monday and I've finished work. It's only fifteen minutes away and from the moment I arrive I'm thinking about getting home, having a shower and brewing my second coffee. I have a wonderful pink cafetière that my husband bought me a few months back after my old one gave out. The filter wouldn't stay attached no matter how much I fiddled with it. Today's choice of coffee is Taylors of Harrogate Hot Lava Java. It's not as strong as I expected given it's marked as a 6 for strength, but my beloved Fika coffee had run out and it wasn't on offer, so Hot Lava Java it was.

A few minutes later, it's brewed and ready to go. I add in some Almond milk, and sit down to enjoy it.

I'm playing catch up with laundry. Our old machine gave up after five and a half years so we had to get another. We got a great deal as it was the Spring Sales, but It took a week to get here, and inevitably it was the week when I took the blankets and cushion covers off of our scatterback sofa, had bath towels lined up to wash, our clothes, my husbands cycling gear and a bunch of cloths and tea towels as well. Our neighbour is a good friend and washed our clothes for me as those needed doing before the new machine got here. I'm slowly getting through it- but I'm limited to what I can fit on the clothes airer and the time it takes things to dry on there. I only tumble dry towels, or else they go hard and are deeply unpleasant to use. Everything else is air dried. Yes it takes longer, but your clothes will last far longer by doing it that way- and it saves so much money. If it's nice out I'll stick the airer on the decking out the back which speeds things up a lot.

I buy Ecover laundry detergent in the 5litre

size. It's cheaper than buying small ones, better for the environment and cleans well. I wash 90% of our stuff on cold wash and it's never a problem. I repurposed an old ketchup squeezy bottle which I decant it into so it's easier to put into the detergent drawer. White Vinegar is a great fabric softener and is naturally anti-bacterial. I use it for towels, as using actual fabric softener makes them hard after a while. For clothes I am a sucker for a nice scent- supermarkets have really upped their game in this department and sell all kinds of scents. I'm partial to summer breeze myself.

Laundry is out, time to press on.

The Kitchen is in need of attention- there are crumbs lurking on the breakfast bar and island that need to go. I sometimes feel like I spend my life wiping crumbs off of the various surfaces in my kitchen! I unload and reload the dishwasher. When we moved in it was the first appliance we bought as I point blank refuse to wash dishes by hand. Other than things that need a soak, or have burnt on food that the dishwasher doesn't really touch- everything goes straight in. I can't bear leaving dirty dishes out overnight. When I go downstairs in the morning I don't want to be greeted by Pyrex in the sink or dirty cutlery. No- in the dishwasher it goes! We don't run ours everyday given its just us two, but we always run the eco wash cycle. It's longer, but its cheaper according to the smart meter. We buy big packs of dishwasher tablets when they are on offer, and use supermarket own brand rinse aid. It works just as well as the name brands! Dishwasher salt is another one- bigger packs are often better value. We use an old 5kg tub under the sink to keep it in.

I wipe down all the surfaces. I just use a cloth and hot soapy water. It does the job without fuss. Everything looks so much better now, and the cloth is thrown in the washing machine.

All that's left is the floor. I saw the underside

of my white socks yesterday and it spurred me on to do this today. A quick hoover with the Shark to pick up all the bits that seem to accumulate, then a good once over with my spin mop. Again, hot soapy water is all I tend to use. From time to time I use actual floor cleaner but I don't necessarily think it does a better job. I also have a flash speed mop for days when it just needs a quick once over.

Chores are done for the day, now it's time to relax for a bit until its time to make dinner.

CHAPTER NINE

A DAY OUT

Husband Is in the office today and I've
decided to have a morning out of the
house. I love being home but as Introverled
as I am, even I need to get out once in a
while.

Our local library is open today. I have a few
books that need returning, and two to
collect. The local library is an unsung hero
and if you're not a member of yours, go join!
The amount of money it has saved me is
incredible. I do pay small amounts to
reserve books from other libraries both in
and out of the county, but it's still cheaper
than buying all the books I borrow. I ordered
a copy of Studio Mcgees interiors book. I
love Studio Mcgee and a part of me wishes
they sold their stuff here, but a part of me is
glad they don't as I'd spend far too much
on everything! It would be lovely to look at

though. I do browse the Target website for fun to see what they have. The reason I'm getting it is that I want to refresh our bedroom. It's been the same for all these years and it's time for a change. I'm doing it on budget (of course) but need some inspiration to give it the Studio Mcgee feel.

The other benefit of joining the library is getting access to the Libby app- which has magazines (from around the world!) e-books, newspapers (if that's your thing) and audiobooks! For free! I love magazines, and occasionally I do buy a paper one for the feel of it. But for the most part I read them on the Libby app. It's available on phone and tablet so I tend to read it on my Kindle as it has the bigger screen so feels more like a magazine.

Our library is run by volunteers as are many in the county due to budget cuts. They are fantastic though and I always have a chat when I go in. I borrow a lot of cookbooks, and they are always keen to hear what I thought, and what I made and they are in agreement that its best to borrow them first to see if it's worth buying. I usually just end up taking a photo on my phone of any recipes I do like and putting them in the recipe album I have on there. I highly recommend this if you love to try new recipes- you can save yourself a lot of money.

It's second coffee time and whilst its brewing I get changed into my indoor clothes. I know there's this whole thing online about wearing good clothes at home and how that is meant to set you up for the day- even wearing makeup as well. I honestly don't get it. I'm just as productive in my comfy clothes as I am in something I'd wear out, and not wearing make-up is my default. I only put make up on on the rare times we are going out somewhere nice that warrants it. I enjoy wearing it but the effort of doing that everyday, and taking it all off again- well, its too much for me. My skincare is as basic as it gets. Wash face in the shower, then apply baby lotion. I've tried all sorts of moisturisers over the years but nothing works for me quite like baby lotion. It leaves my skin soft and doesn't make It red or cause it to break out like everything else I've tried. I also have a cleansing balm that I reserve for taking off makeup as it gets rid of mascara easily. Its the W7 Peachy Keen- £5 from Amazon- it smells lush and is vegan and cruelty free.

I pour over the pages of the Studio Mcgee book. Everything is so perfect. But also too perfect. There's no life in these pictures. No books on shelves, no remote controls on the sofa, no appliances anywhere! I have to remind myself that these are staged photos, they don't represent day to day living. I've gotten the necessary inspiration and I know what I'm after to recreate the look. The challenge begins- finding what I would like to have without spending a fortune! That's for another day though- this is a slow project.

CHAPTER TEN

PIZZA AND NETFLIX

It's Pizza night! Every Wednesday we enjoy homemade pizza for dinner. My husband could eat pizza several times a week- it's one of his favourites (he loves cheese) but we stick to once a week for the sake of our waistlines.

I pop the ingredients for the dough in the bread maker. It only takes 45minutes to come together. After that I split the dough in half and place It on a pizza tray to prove it. I use the oven to proof dough and it works every time. Put a Pyrex filled with boiling water on the bottom, then put the tray with dough on the top and close the door quickly. I leave mine for an hour- they puff up perfectly! I roll and shape them into two bases and part bake one to have for the following week since we share one (They are big as a thin base pizza)

I make the pizza sauce too- simmer Passtata, Garlic, 60ml of beer, 1/2tsp of Sugar and some Basil and Oregano for about 30minutes on low. I freeze what I don't use as it makes enough for two pizzas. You can leave the beer out, but it does make it extra tasty.

I don't make the cheese- even I'm not that industrious! We each make our own pizza half- mainly because I love vegan pepperoni and he hates it. 15 minutes later, and dinner is served.

After dinner we watch exactly one episode of something on a streaming service- usually sci fi or sci fi adjacent. We don't binge watch anything. Honestly- I'd get too fidgety! After we've watched whatever it is we like to just read and relax the rest of the evening.

There's no TV in our house so no Sky, Virgin or

any of those services. They're expensive and honestly nothing on them remotely appeals to us. If you're looking to simplify and cut costs- this would be a great place to start. Most people watch hours of TV everyday- if you remove or reduce your package, you could get back so many hours to do something else with!

CHAPTER ELEVEN

BATHROOM CLEANING

Thursday is bathroom and bedroom clean day. It doesn't take long as I stay on top of it. I love Ocean Saver Pomegranate Bathroom spray. You buy the bottle, then the refill tablets which you put in the bottle when the spray is gone, and add water. They were on offer for £1 recently so I stocked up. I also have HG Limescale spray- because this is the South of England and the water is HARD. Sometimes I have to use this spray to really cut though the worst of the limescale that nothing else will touch.

For the toilet I use disinfectant wipes. Not the most eco friendly option, but I *cannot* deal with using a cloth for this job. Everyone has their limits- and that's mine. I love the Fabulosa wipes- especially the winter angel scent, which smells just like Snow Fairy from

Lush. They are just a few pounds, and a pack lasts me ages as I only use them for the toilet. Once everything has been scrubbed I run the hoover to pick up stray hairs and other bits, then a quick mop (our bathroom is tiny) and it's done! The main bedroom is equally quick- we only have 2 bedside tables, a chest of drawers and a shelf in there as the wardrobes and linen cupboard are built in. So dusting is quick. My husbands office and my library/office/reading room take a little longer as they have more surfaces and things that need moving to dust properly. I always finish with hoovering to collect the dust that has inevitably fallen to the floor. All in all I'd day this takes me from an hour, to an hour and a half which I think is pretty quick for the amount of rooms. As always, if you stay on top of it- it won't take as long. Keeping the clutter at bay helps too.

CHAPTER TWELVE

USED BOOKS

My book came today. I ordered The Beach Lovers Retreat by Heidi Swain. I got a used, very good condition copy with postage for under £3! I know this is a book I'll probably only read once on our upcoming holiday, so a used copy that I will then donate once I'm done, made sense.

Last year I was on a quest to re-purchase books that I had lost in my many moves over the years. Specifically- book series I had loved as a teenager and wanted to re-read. As a child of the 90s/00s I grew up on witchy tv- Charmed, Sabrina, Buffy, etc and I was big into witchy fiction books. I found used copies of all the series I wanted across a few months. Most of them were long since out of print, so used was really my only option. My bookcase now has an entire shelf devoted to "teen reads" and I love it! I'll be honest, some of them held up more than others- but the nostalgia is priceless.

World of Books is my go to for used books. The condition described is always accurate- I've had books from other places which were definitely more "acceptable" than very good! You can find them on eBay, and they also sell on Amazon Marketplace.

If you're buying used books on eBay- do check to see if the seller is a library. I say this because if they are, you are going to be getting an ex library book with the dewey decimal sticker on the spine and the library sticker on the inside cover- which not everyone is keen on. I personally think its fun!

Charity shops are of course another great source for used books, and you can take them home there are then, rather than waiting for the post to arrive. However, as I was looking for very specific books it wasn't my go to on that occasion. You have to be a bit more open minded at the Charity shop. Its useful to keep list of authors you enjoy on your phone so you can easily check whether they have them or not. Cookbooks are one of the best charity shop finds. You can save so much money, as they are typically hardback so they were expensive to begin with- now they can be yours for just a few pounds. I always find memoirs are a popular subject too- if that's your thing.

CHAPTER THIRTEEN

BOOKS AND BAKING

A leisurely start to the day for me, I woke up at 7am (which almost never happens) made a coffee and sat downstairs for about an hour. I did a brief check of the headlines (I wish I hadn't) and downloaded an e-book that I had meant to do yesterday, but got caught up in something else and forgot.

The e book was *A Feast of Life*, by Kate Singh. Kate is the queen of frugal, and her chatty style makes you feel like you're having a coffee with a friend She lives in North California with her husband and two sons, and they get by, with ease, on her husbands humble salary of about $15 an hour. They own their own home, and Kate is a stay at home mum. She's written over ten books detailing her experiences and tips- I highly recommend them if you love all things frugal living. You might have to google a few things if you aren't American to get a full understanding, but they are well worth a read.

I'm making Oatmeal Sultana Chocolate Chip cookies- as we have tons of oats, a giant bag of sultanas from Costco and a few half opened bags of chocolate chips that needed using up. I pretty much always bake our cookies/muffins/cakes from scratch. I like knowing what's in it, and the whole process for me is meditative. It doesn't always work out cheaper- but then again I'm not using things like dirt cheap palm oil. To me, it's worth it as I'm using better quality ingredients, but I certainly don't begrudge anyone buying a pack of supermarket own brand biscuits for £1.

CHAPTER FOURTEEN

SUNDAY WRITING

Sundays are always quiet here.

I like to catch up on my writing on Sundays, and aim to have a blog post published on Monday, and another later in the week. Of course, I'm also busy writing the book you are currently reading!

I've always loved writing. When I was younger I used to make my own little magazines. I would write the "stories" come up with the headlines and do all the illustrations. Once it was done I would staple them together and admire my efforts!

In my teens I had a brief stint of poetry writing. One of my teachers liked a poem I had written so much that she had me read it in front of our year assembly, which was pretty nerve wracking but it was over in a few minutes. My foray into poetry didn't last long, and to this day I'm still not really into it.

What I do love though is non fiction! Of course, I love a fiction book as much as the next person but I love non fiction for the chance to learn something new, to read about some aspect of someone's life or just to gather useful tips and information on a practical subject.

Writing gives me a creative outlet. Whilst I'm not sure I would ever turn my hand to writing fiction, what I do love is sharing parts of my life that I think could help or inspire others in some way.

Writing is a fantastic low cost hobby to have, and a way to while the hours away at home on a leisurely Sunday- or whatever day works for you. There's plenty of free resources online to hep you improve your writing, and I highly recommend *Stephen*

King- On Writing to anyone looking to get started. Reading books on writing however, is no substitute for *actually* getting started. The more you write, the better your writing becomes. NanNoWriMo can be a fun way to challenge yourself. It's an online challenge to write 50k words in a mo
nth (November is the main one, but there's also one in April I believe) You don't have to have a finished or polished book by the end, but it's a great motivator!

CHAPTER FIFTEEN

SPRING MARKET

Our local garden centre had their annual Spring Market today. It's free entry, and has stalls with local craftspeople showing off their wares. My husband loves a garden centre trip (This is a sure sign one had reached elder millennial status!) so we jumped in the car and took a drive.

This is a small independent garden centre, and it is charming! All the stalls had been set up in the outdoor walled garden area and it was fun to walk around and see what they had. I had said to myself before we left that I could treat myself to something small. It's important to set limits at these events or else you can quickly find yourself out of pocket!

There were stalls selling pottery, jewellery, alcohol, crystals- all sorts! I came across a stall selling the aforementioned crystals, as well as incense and other "new age" type goodies and saw they had little pouches of bath soaks- which also contained little crystals! There was one for confidence, one for positivity, and one for calm. I picked confidence- mostly because it had rose petals but also, we could all use a confidence boost from time to time, right? They came with little bags that you put a scoopful into (don't want to flush crystals down the drain!) and it was only £4.50. One tap of the debit card later, and it was mine! I was happy that I had resisted the urge to buy all the beautiful things, and has kept to my resolve to only buy one small thing.

Once I'd finished perusing the stalls we headed back to the main garden centre area. There was a gorgeous tree, but at £150 we snapped a picture of the tag to see if maybe in the future we could find a smaller potting to grow ourselves and save on the cost of buying a fully mature tree. We opted for the 3 for £9.99 offer on the 9cm perennials. When it comes to plants I have 2 criteria- the appearance and the name. I let my husband check if the plant is actually suitable for our garden. I found a little plant called the "Magic Rose" that was pink, and after he checked it would be ok for our garden- in the basket it went! He planted it that same day, and I'm really hoping it takes root and thrives as it's so pretty.

CHAPTER SIXTEEN

BAKING BREAD

It's a grey wet day outside. It may be May, but it doesn't feel like it on days like this!

Baking bread is always fun, but on days like this it just feels like the perfect thing to do. I find it quite meditative- even though I use a bread maker and thus don't do any actual kneading. Measuring out the ingredients, adding them in in the correct order- it's calming somehow.

Today I'm making Maple Pecan Bread. This and my Spicy Fruit Loaf are my two favourite "special" recipes to make. They both make excellent toast slathered in dairy free spread! It's not a quick process- it takes 5hours from the minute you set it going, but most of that time is resting. Resting allows the ingredients to emulsify properly, resulting in a much better loaf. Plus I don't have to do anything with it, a case of set it and forget it- until it beeps!

I found a recipe the other day for Swedish Cardamom Buns, know as *Kardemummabullar* buns in Sweden. They are similar to Cinnamon buns in terms of making them, but they have a delicious sweet and spicy taste. I have a small jar of Cardamom languishing in the cupboard, so I'll definitely be having a go at making these soon. I'll use the dough setting on the bread maker to do the heavy lifting so to speak, but I will need to shape and bake them by hand. This will definitely call for watching a YouTube video as I read the instructions on shaping them and can't make head nor tails of them!

CHAPTER SEVENTEEN

THE ISLAND OF LOVE

Today is a very exciting day- we are off to Cyprus for a belated Honeymoon (We got married in Lockdown, so very belated!) We have never actually had a proper holiday the whole time we have been together, so I'm excited for our first one!

We booked an early flight at 6am- that way we won't miss out on a whole day. Plus I'm a morning person anyway, I had no qualms about being on the airport shuttle bus at 2.45am!

I splurged on some new clothes for this trip because I didn't have a lot of Summer clothes to begin with, and only one bikini! I'm not a big fan of shopping these days- I do it all online, and I seem to be lucky with it as I've never had to return anything!

We had a fantastic week. We went all inclusive and it was worth every penny. No having to worry about the cost of eating out, or finding somewhere to eat! There wasn't the widest choice of vegetarian food some days, but we made do. And what they lacked in the main course I more than made up for in desert!

Not one for simply lounging around, we did a few trips. The Archaeological site, the Zoo, the Waterpark and the Old Town. Needless to say we got our steps in. I let my Bellabeat tracker at home for fear of losing it. At £250 worth of tech, I wasn't going to risk it! Apple health tracks steps though, so I could still check that.

What I love most about being on holiday (other than the instant dopamine hit of the sun hitting your face as you step off the plane!) is that the distance between there and home gives you space to think and reflect. Maybe it's just the sun and blue skies, but I get filled with a sense of "I can change anything I want to!"- similar to New Years I think. I definitely want more of this- travelling. I hadn't left the country for over fifteen years prior to this trip, but now I'm remembering what it feels like to be somewhere else, a different culture, climate, people- all of it!

Our next trip will be a city break to Copenhagen, Denmark. If you've read my last book you'll know I'm a teeny tiny bit obsessed with all things hygge- and seeing as that originates from Denmark it seems the logical thing to do is to visit, and learn more. Plus its only a two hour flight from here, I have no excuses.

Next year I definitely want another beach holiday of sorts. Not sure where, but a yearly dose of palm trees and blue skies is in order me thinks.

CHAPTER EIGHTEEN

ON WRITING

They say everyone needs a hobby, an outlet. Something that is fun, creative and doesn't have to be monetised (unless you want to!)

For me, that's writing. I mentioned this briefly in part one, but let's dig into it a bit deeper.

Writing is a much needed outlet from work and keeping house. We don't have children, so keeping house doesn't take up all my time, nor does my part time job. I have the luxury of time, and this is how I choose to spend it.

It was never my dream to be a famous author- fame of any kind is not for me. I write mostly for myself, and only found the confidence to start a blog and write my first short book a few years ago. I fell in love with the short book format popularised by the likes of Fiona Ferris, Kate Singh and Jennifer Melville. I liked the fact there's no waffle- they are to the point and, to quote a famous advert, do exactly what they say on the tin! Non fiction is my preference for writing, but I have written some short fictional stories for fun. I don't have the imagination or patience for novel writing. The endless descriptions, character reflections, monologues. I just can't! I skim over that in most books I read, so I certainly couldn't write it.

I love brewing a cup of coffee, turning on my laptop and just cracking on. I write, and do my best not to self edit until the end. I typically write about a subject I'm feeling interested in that day, then I simply move various paragraphs around so it flows more easily, and makes sense.

I prefer to write in the mornings, but that doesn't always happen. Its currently 15:05 as I write this, and my brain is slowly shutting down. I just had a few thoughts I needed to get down, but this is not a great time for me to write much of anything!

CHAPTER NINETEEN

ITS HYGGE TIME

It seems like every man and his dog is talking about hygge online these days. I've been a bit obsessed for a few years now, and my last book Cosy Autumn was inspired by my love of it.

This year, we are taking it one step further and *actually going* to the home of hygge-Denmark! Two holidays In one year, after six years together and not leaving the country-clearly we are making up for lost time. Also- I turn 40 this year, so we can chalk this extravagance up to that milestone!

We got a great deal for a 3 night stay. I'm mildly terrified of flying with Ryanair though-I've never flown with them, but their reputation precedes them. Its only 2 hours mind, I'm sure It will be fine!

In the spirit of simplicity and frugality though we won't be doing anything too lavish. No Michelin starred dinners (Though tbh that's the last thing I'd ever want to do, anywhere) Instead we will be checking out the local bakeries for breakfast and foodhalls for lunch and dinner. Copenhagen is notoriously expensive, but with careful planning and research I'm confident we can do it on a sensible budget. If all else fails we can take a trip to the local Netto or Lidl!

Denmark has a great scheme- The Copenhagen Card, which for a set fee gives you entry to all the tourist attractions, and access to public transport! Such a great idea, and very helpful from a budget perspective. It doesn't include entry to the rides at Tivoli Gardens, but you can purchase that separately.

CHAPTER TWENTY

A DAY OUT IN THE COUNTRY

This past weekend we took a trip to one of our favourite National Trust sites- Avebury. Situated in Wiltshire, which is only 90mins drive for us, it's a wonderfully peaceful place- and has the worlds largest stone circle. Its far quieter than Stonehenge, far bigger and you can touch the stones (which you can't at Stonehenge) There are also other neolithic sites in walking distance including Silbury Hill (which you can walk around, but not on top of due to erosion) and West Kennet Long Barrow, which is an ancient burial site with chambers you can walk into.

We started with West Kennet, as we didn't have time on our last visit. We got there early as the only parking is a lay by, and by the time we finished mid-morning, it was full! Its an uphill walk, though not too steep- but it was well worth it. There were Swallows everywhere- diving down and flying back up, and my husband got some excellent shots on his DSLR camera. We wondered around the chambers (very small, but still worth a visit) and found lots of pagan offerings/spellwork. Avebury is definitely a pilgrimage site for Pagans, and there is definitely a local community here given the landscape and history.

We then headed to the main car park to explore the stone circle. Avebury is free to enter whether you're a member or not. There is a fee to visit the manor house, gardens and museum if you're not a member but the scenery is so perfect you don't necessarily need to visit those places, unless you want to of course.

We wandered around the fields- these are active grazing land so expect to see sheep and cows as you walk. I'd advise walking boots or shoes as the ground is uneven and sometimes stony. Of course, being a grazing field its also full of you-know-what, so wear a different pair of shoes at least in case you step in something! And remember, you're a visitor in these fields, do not disturb or get close to the animals. They are used to visitors and will generally stay out of your way.

We bought a picnic with us to avoid buying food at the cafe- mostly because the vegetarian options can be limiting, and also because it gets very busy. There was a 3 for 2 offer on Quorn picnic foods that week- bonus! I also made us some sandwiches and cooked some mini sausage rolls. There are lots of picnic benches- which is just as well as you do not want to lay a picnic blanket in the fields, due to the aforementioned issue! There's something very nostalgic and comforting about picnics. When I was young we often took a picnic when we went on day trips. My nan would always cook cocktail sausages and wrap them in brown paper- I can still see her clear as day in my mind carefully unwrapping them when we sat down to eat. My brother still

has the tartan picnic rug we sat on!
After a good few hours, and about 11,000
steps we were ready to go. Tired, but happy
to have had a wonderful day out!

IN CONCLUSION

I really hope you've enjoyed this book- both the tips section, and my meanderings of everyday life that show how we live simply, and enjoy the everyday.

For more, come follow me on Instagram @melaniesteeleauthor

ABOUT THE AUTHOR

Melanie Steele (she/her) is a late thirty (almost forty!) something living in a cosy village in Buckinghamshire with her Husband. You'll most often find her in the Kitchen baking a recipe she found online on her phone, then cursing herself for not turning auto timeout off and thus getting her phone covered in flour when the screen goes black.

You can find her on Instagram @melaniesteeleauthor

Printed in Great Britain
by Amazon

47439396R00056